Around the World in Eighty Days

STARTER LEVEL   **250 HEADWORDS**

OXFORD
UNIVERSITY PRESS

Great Clarendon Street, Oxford OX2 6DP

Oxford University Press is a department of the University of Oxford.
It furthers the University's objective of excellence in research, scholarship,
and education by publishing worldwide in

Oxford New York

Auckland Cape Town Dar es Salaam Hong Kong Karachi
Kuala Lumpur Madrid Melbourne Mexico City Nairobi
New Delhi Shanghai Taipei Toronto

With offices in

Argentina Austria Brazil Chile Czech Republic France Greece
Guatemala Hungary Italy Japan Poland Portugal Singapore
South Korea Switzerland Thailand Turkey Ukraine Vietnam

OXFORD and OXFORD ENGLISH are registered trade marks of
Oxford University Press in the UK and in certain other countries

This edition © Oxford University Press 2010

ISBN: 978 0 19 424701 6 BOOK
ISBN: 978 0 19 424665 1 BOOK AND MULTIROM PACK
MULTIROM NOT AVAILABLE SEPARATELY

ACKNOWLEDGEMENTS

Illustrations by: Mark Draisey (main story), Mark Ruffle (p49).

The publisher would like to thank the following for permission to reproduce photographs:

Cover: Getty Images (elephant through arch/Ed Freeman/The Image Bank)

Alamy Images p 19 (Indian Princess/Popperfoto); ATM Images pp 44 (Helicopter), 44
(Jeep); David Noble Photolibrary p 43 (Tower Bridge/Laurie Noble); Getty Images pp 43
(Penguins/Frans Lemmens), 44 (Mountain biking/John Kelly), 44 (Jet ski/Mike Brinson);
Hutchison Picture Library pp 43 (Amazon rainforest/Jesco von Puttkamer), 43 (Mount
Everest), 44 (Ferry in Peru/Edward Parker); ImageState p 43 (Sydney Opera House); Mary
Evans Picture Library p 39 (Wedding); OUP p iv (Elephant/Photodisc); iv (liner/Photodisc),
iv (Car/Photodisc), iv (Man on bike/Photodisc), 13 (Men talking/Photodisc), 43 (New York/
Photodisc), 44 (Train/Digital Vision), 44 (Savannah/Corbis), 44 (Aeroplane/Photodisc), 44
(Hang glider/Photodisc).

DOMINOES

Series Editors: Bill Bowler and Sue Parminter

Around the World in Eighty Days

Jules Verne

Text adaptation by Bill Bowler

Illustrated by Mark Draisey

Jules Verne (1828–1905) was born in Nantes, France, and he started to write for the theatre when he was a student in Paris. His first novel was *Five Weeks in a Balloon* (1862), and he went on to write more than sixty other science fiction and adventure books. He became one of the most famous writers of his time.

OXFORD
UNIVERSITY PRESS

BEFORE READING

1 Match the words with the pictures.

balloon
bicycle
camel
car
elephant
horse and carriage
ship
train

2 The story happens in 1872. How do people move from country to country?

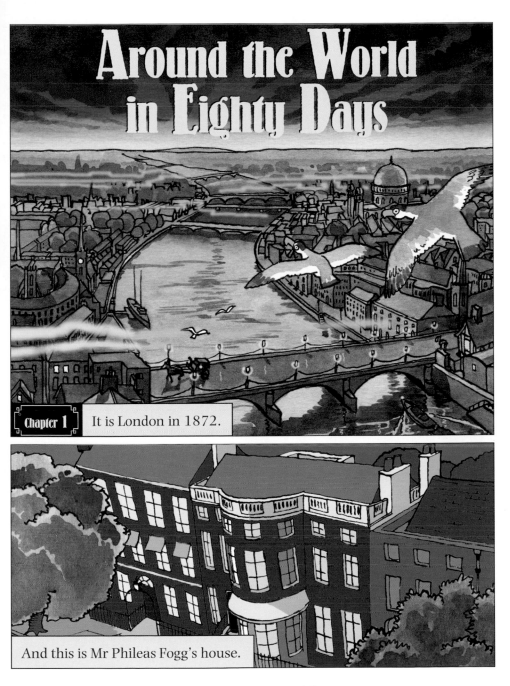

Around the World in Eighty Days

Chapter 1 It is London in 1872.

And this is Mr Phileas Fogg's house.

around all the way round

world where we all live; people live in lots of different countries in the world

Mr Phileas Fogg is an English **gentleman**. He lives in London.

He hasn't got a wife or children, but he has got a French **servant** – **Passepartout**.

Fogg goes to his **club** every day.

GENTLEMAN'S CLUB

He eats at his club at 12 o'clock. In the afternoon he reads there. In the evening he eats there again. Then he talks with his friends, and at midnight he goes home.

gentleman a man from a rich family who does not need to work

servant a person who works for someone rich

club a place where gentlemen meet

Passepartout /ˈpæspaːˌtuː/

Passepartout is happy. He wants a quiet job.

Mr. Fogg's day:
8.00: gets up
8.23: breakfast
9.37: gets ready
11.30: goes to club
midnight: goes home

But one evening, Fogg sees something interesting in *The Times*.

THE TIMES

GENTLEMAN THIEF TAKES £5,000 FROM THE BANK OF ENGLAND.

At the club Fogg's friends talk.
'That gentleman **thief** can't go far,' says Ralph.
'With trains and **ships**, today's **detectives** move fast.'
'But thieves can move fast too,' Flanagan says.

bank people put money and expensive things here

thief (*plural* **thieves**) a person who takes things without asking

ship you use a ship to go across the water

detective a special policeman

'Today you can go round the world in eighty days,' says Fogg.

'Do it, and I pay you £20,000,' says Stuart.

'I'm leaving tonight,' answers Fogg. 'Perhaps I *can't* do it, Stuart. But then I pay *you* £20,000.'

The train for France leaves before nine in the evening. Fogg must be back in London by 21st December.

Fogg gives £20,000 in a bag to his servant. 'We're leaving for France.' he says. Passepartout isn't very happy.

They go to France. Then they take a train to Italy, and a ship to **Port Said** in Egypt.

When their ship arrives in Suez, an English detective – Mr Fix – is waiting. He's looking for the gentleman thief.

Fogg visits the **passport** office.

Mr Fix sees him there. 'It's the gentleman thief!' he thinks. 'I must tell London.'

Port Said /ˌpɔːt ˈsaɪd/

passport a book with your name and photograph; you take it with you when you visit different countries

READING CHECK

**1 Are these sentences true or false?
Tick the boxes.**

	True	False
a Phileas Fogg has got children.	☐	☑
b Passepartout wants a quiet job.	☐	☐
c Fogg takes £50,000 from the Bank of England.	☐	☐
d He wants to go round the world in 80 days.	☐	☐
e He leaves London on 21st December.	☐	☐
f He gives £20,000 to his servant.	☐	☐
g Passepartout is happy to go round the world.	☐	☐
h Fix is in Egypt when Fogg arrives there.	☐	☐

2 Match the names with the jobs and the pictures.

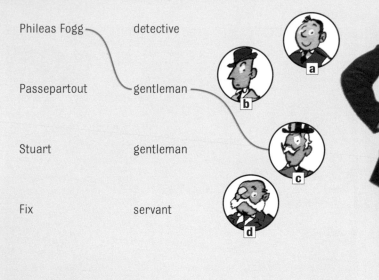

Phileas Fogg — detective

Passepartout — gentleman

Stuart — gentleman

Fix — servant

WORD WORK

Match the sentences with the words from Chapter 1.

a Phileas Fogg is a . . . .

b You can use this to go across the sea.

c A . . . takes money and other things from people.

d Sherlock Holmes is a famous . . . .

e A small 'book' that you need to go from one country to another country.

f Passepartout is Phileas Fogg's . . . .

g Fogg wants to go around the . . . in eighty days.

h A special building with a lot of money in it.

i Fogg usually eats here.

j Fogg is going . . . the world.

bank
around
thief
servant
passport
detective
ship
world
gentleman
club

GUESS WHAT

What does Detective Fix do in the next chapter?
Complete the sentences with the best words.

a He talks to . . . . | Fogg | Passepartout | the Bank

b He goes . . . . | to a shop | home | to the airport

c He . . . London. | phones | writes to | goes to

d He . . . Egypt. | leaves | visits | stays in

e He . . . Fogg. | stays with | stops | forgets

Chapter 2

Fix looks at Passepartout.
'Where are you going?' he asks.
'Around the world,' says
Passepartout. 'But right now
I need some new shirts.'

Fix takes him to a shop and leaves him there.

Then he sends a **telegram** to London.

Later he gets on the ship for Bombay with Fogg and Passepartout.

telegram a very short letter that you send very quickly

It is 20th October. They all arrive in Bombay – two days early. At 4.30 in the afternoon, Fogg and Passepartout leave the ship. They want to get a train across India to Calcutta. It leaves at 8 o'clock.

First Fogg goes to the passport office. Then he eats at the **station**.

Passepartout visits the **temple** at Malcbar Hill . . . . . . but he doesn't take off his shoes.

The **priests** get angry. They take his shoes and Passepartout runs away.

station people get on and off trains here   **temple** some people go here to pray   **priest** a man who works in a temple

Fogg and Passepartout get on the train, but Fix stays in Bombay. He is waiting for a telegram from London.

After three days the train stops. The **railway** from Kholby to Allahabad isn't ready.

Some men are **building** the railway. But there are 80 kilometres without a railway between Kholby and Allahabad.

In Kholby, Passepartout gets some new shoes. He also finds an **elephant** to take them to Allahabad.

They stop near a temple in the village of Pillaji. The old Indian **prince** is dead. His young wife, the **princess**, must die with him in a big **fire**.

'We must help that woman!' says Fogg.

---

railway a train moves on this

build to make something like a house or a railway

elephant a very big animal with a long nose

prince the most important man in a little country

princess the wife of a prince

fire this is red and hot, and it burns

The priests start the fire. Through the smoke Fogg sees something beautiful. The prince stands up and takes the princess out of the fire.

The prince and the princess come nearer. Fogg sees that the man is not the prince. It is Passepartout in the prince's **clothes**.
'Quickly! Let's go!' says Passepartout to Fogg, quietly.

Suddenly the priests see the prince's body on the fire. They see that the man in the prince's clothes is not the prince, and they become angry.

Fogg, Passepartout and the princess leave very quickly on the elephant.

clothes people wear these

READING CHECK

1 Put these sentences in the correct order. Number them 1–6.

a Passepartout and Fogg get on a train. ☐ U

b Passepartout, Fogg and Fix get on a ship. ☐ I

c Passepartout gets new shoes and finds an elephant. ☐ N

d Passepartout goes to a temple and loses his shoes. ☐ O

e Passepartout helps a young woman. ☐ I

f Passepartout and Fix speak. ☐1 Ⓚ

2 Complete the table to find the elephant's name.

1	2	3	4	5	6
K					

WORD WORK

Find the words for these pictures in the wordsquare.

T	E	P	Q	R	V	P	C	P	R
E	L	E	P	H	A	N	T	R	X
L	X	T	E	M	P	L	E	I	D
E	M	G	R	O	R	Y	T	N	C
G	S	T	A	T	I	O	N	C	L
R	O	F	I	R	E	E	F	E	O
A	A	L	L	R	S	P	U	S	T
M	S	L	W	W	T	J	B	S	H
M	Z	K	A	P	R	I	N	C	E
C	I	O	Y	V	D	I	L	C	S

GUESS WHAT

1 **What happens next? Join the words to make sentences about the next chapter.**

1 Fogg	**a**	see Passepartout's shoes again	**f**	in Hong Kong.
2 Fogg, Passepartout and the Princess	**b**	slowly falls in love	**g**	in Calcutta.
3 Passepartout and Fogg	**c**	have a drink together	**h**	with the princess.
4 Fogg and Passepartout	**d**	leave the elephant	**i**	on a ship going to Hong Kong.
5 Fix and Passepartout	**e**	take the princess to a friend	**j**	in Hong Kong.

2 **Write out the sentences.**

1 Fogg slowly falls in love with the princess.

2

3

4

5

Chapter 3 At last they arrive in Allahabad.

Fogg **buys** some European clothes for the princess. 'What a beautiful woman!' he thinks.

On the train going to Calcutta, she speaks for the first time. 'My name's Mrs Aouda. Thank you for helping me! But I don't know what to do now. I can never go home!'

'We can take you to Hong Kong,' Fogg says.
'Thank you,' says Mrs Aouda.
'I have a **cousin** there.'

buy to give money for something

cousin the son (or daughter) of your father's (or mother's) brother (or sister)

At Calcutta station a policeman stops them. He takes them to see a **judge**. Mrs Aouda goes too.

Fix is in Calcutta. (Detectives must move fast to find gentlemen thieves.) He's waiting in **court**, but Fogg and his friends don't see him.

'Why are we here?'
'For **breaking the rules** in a temple,' says the judge.

'In Pillaji?' asks Fogg.
'No! In Bombay!' says the judge. And he puts Passepartout's shoes on the table.

judge a person who says when something is right or wrong

court a judge works here

breaking the rules doing the things that people must not do

'You must go to **prison** for this,' says the judge. But Fogg gives two thousand pounds to the court and they're **free** again.

They get onto the ship for Hong Kong. Fix **follows** them, but Passepartout sees him.
'Perhaps he's a detective,' he thinks.
'Perhaps he's working for Mr Stuart from the Gentleman's Club in London.'

In Hong Kong, Mrs Aouda learns that her cousin now lives in Holland. 'Come with us to Europe,' Fogg says.

6th Nov.

---

prison a place where people must stay when they do something wrong

free not in prison

follow to go after someone

Passepartout wants to buy three tickets on the *Carnatic*. It leaves for Yokohama, in Japan, the next morning. But at the ticket office he learns that it's leaving early – that evening.

Passepartout meets Fix near the ticket office. 'Come for a drink,' says Fix.

Fix tells Passepartout, 'I think your Mr Fogg is a gentleman thief and I want to **arrest** him.' Passepartout doesn't want to help Fix, but the detective buys drink after drink.

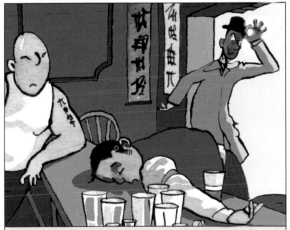

Passepartout goes to sleep on the table. 'Now he can't tell Fogg about the *Carnatic*,' thinks Fix. 'It leaves tonight – but without Fogg!'

arrest to take someone to court or to prison

READING CHECK

Choose the correct pictures.

a Fogg gives
the princess . . .

1⃣ 2⃣ 3⃣

b Who meets them
at Calcutta station?

1⃣ 2⃣ 3⃣

c In Calcutta
they nearly go to . . .

1⃣ 2⃣ 3⃣

d The ship to Japan
leaves on . . .

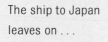

1⃣ 2⃣ 3⃣

e Who doesn't want
Fogg to get the *Carnatic*?

1⃣ 2⃣ 3⃣

ACTIVITIES

WORD WORK

1 Find the words. They are all in Chapter 3.

cousin _____

_____ _____

_____

2 Write the words from Activity 1 in the sentences.

a Fogg pays £2000 not to go to ...prison.. .

b Mrs Aouda's .... lives in Holland.

c Fix ....s Fogg to Calcutta.

d Fogg doesn't see Fix in the ....

e Fix wants to .... Fogg.

GUESS WHAT

What happens in the next chapter?
Tick the boxes.

	Yes	No
a Passepartout goes to Japan on the *Carnatic*.	☐	☐
b Fogg goes to Japan on the *Carnatic*.	☐	☐
c Fix makes friends with Passepartout.	☐	☐
d Fix goes to Japan with Fogg.	☐	☐
e Passepartout works in a Japanese hotel.	☐	☐
f Fogg can't find Passepartout in Japan.	☐	☐
g In Japan they get a ship to England.	☐	☐

Later Passepartout **wakes up**. He goes onto the *Carnatic* and the ship leaves, but Fogg and Mrs Aouda aren't with him.

Next morning Fogg and Mrs Aouda go to get on the *Carnatic*. But it isn't there.

Fix arrives. 'The *Carnatic*'s **on its way** to Japan,' he says. 'And the next ship to Yokohama leaves next week.'

'Where's Passepartout?' asks Mrs Aouda.
'I don't know,' says Fogg. 'But we must go on without him. We must find another ship!'

wake up to stop sleeping   **on its way** going

Fogg finds a small ship – the *Tankadere* – to go to Shanghai. There they can get a big ship to Yokohama.
'Can I go with you?' asks Fix.
'Of course,' Fogg answers.

The *Tankadere* **travels** through **storms**...

...and at last arrives near Shanghai.

Suddenly they see a big ship in front of them. It's on its way to Yokohama. '**Signal** to that ship,' says Fogg.

travel to go

storm a lot of rain and very bad weather

signal to talk from ship to ship

Passepartout arrives in Yokohama, but he has no money. He leaves the *Carnatic* and finds work in Mr Batulcar's **circus**. 'I can go to America with the circus,' he thinks.

Fogg, Mrs Aouda and Fix get on the big ship and a week later they arrive in Japan.

The *Carnatic* is in Yokohama. Fogg and Mrs Aouda go onto the *Carnatic*. They find Passepartout's name in the book of **passengers**' names, but they can't find Passepartout.

circus an exciting show

passenger someone who travels on a ship or train

Their ship leaves for San Francisco in a few hours. Before they leave, Fogg goes to the circus.

Passepartout sees him there. 'Mr Fogg!' he says happily.

Fogg wants to take Passepartout with him. But first he must **pay** Mr Batulcar.

At 6 o'clock in the evening Fogg, Passepartout and Mrs Aouda go onto the American ship. Fix follows them.

pay to give money for something

READING CHECK

Use the words in the balloons to write sentences about Chapter 4.

leaves
gets
finds
go
sees
all

go to Yokohama
Passepartout
the *Carnatic*
the circus
work in
by ship

a circus
to Japan
on another ship
with Fogg
to America
at the Circus

a Passepartout .gets the Carnatic to Japan .
b Fogg, Mrs Aouda and Fix …………………………………… .
c Passepartout …………………………………… .
d Fogg …………………………………… .
e Passepartout …………………………………… .
f Fogg, Mrs Aouda, Passepartout and Fix …………………………………… .

WORD WORK

1 Find the words from Chapter 4 in the railway.

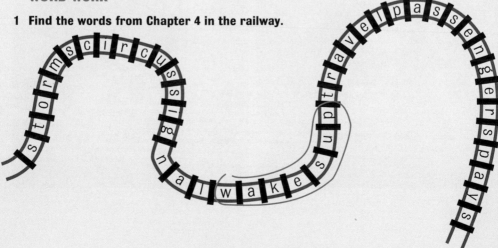

2 Write the words from Activity 1 in the sentences.

   a Passepartout .*wakes up.* and goes onto the *Carnatic.*

   b Fogg, Fix and Mrs Aouda .... to China on a small ship.

   c There are bad .... as they go from India to China.

   d They .... to a big ship.

   e Mr Batulcar has a ....

   f Fogg .... Mr Batulcar some money.

   g Passepartout's name is on the list of .... on the *Carnatic.*

GUESS WHAT

What happens in the next chapter? Tick three boxes.

   a Fix arrests Fogg. ☐

   c Passepartout fights some Indians. ☐

   b Fix helps Fogg. ☐

   d They get a train to New York. ☐

'I'm sorry about Hong Kong,' says Passepartout. 'I don't usually drink much, but . . .'

Later Passepartout sees Fix on the ship. 'My master isn't a gentleman thief,' he says.

'Listen,' says Fix. 'I now have **papers** from London to arrest Mr Fogg. But I can't stop him now. It must be in England. When we get there . . .'

They arrive in San Francisco in the morning. The New York train leaves that evening.

Fogg and Mrs Aouda meet Fix in the street. 'I am travelling to Europe now. Can we travel together?' he asks. 'Of course,' answers Fogg.

papers letters, usually from an important person

They walk into a **meeting**. 'Camerfield for judge!' **shout** the people on the left. 'Mandiboy for judge!' shout the people on the right.

Then they start **fighting**. One man wants to fight Fogg but Fix stands in front of him and stops him.

Passepartout finds it all very strange. 'So, Mr Fix is helping us now!' he thinks.

Fogg, Mrs Aouda, Passepartout and Fix get on the train that evening.

meeting when a number of people come to talk about something important

shout to say loudly and angrily

fight to hit someone again and again

They cross one old bridge very fast and it **falls** into the **river** behind them.

Then some Sioux Indians arrive. They kill some passengers. Passepartout fights them . . .

. . . but they take him and **ride** away with him.

Fogg, Mrs Aouda and Fix get off the train.

fall to go down suddenly

river water that moves through the country in a long line

ride to go on a horse

Fogg goes to look for Passepartout.

He finds him and brings him back. But they must wait until evening, until the next train to New York.

'How can we travel fast over the **snow**?' thinks Fix. On a **sledge** with **sails**!

Soon they arrive in Omaha. There they take a train to New York.

They arrive in New York 45 minutes late! Their ship – the *China* – is on its way to Liverpool.

snow something soft, cold and white

sledge something for travelling on snow

sail this uses wind to help something move

READING CHECK

Choose the right words to finish the sentences.

a On the ship to America . . .
  1 ☐ Mrs Aouda talks to Fix.
  2 ☐ Fogg sees Fix.
  3 ☑ Passepartout talks to Fix.

b Fix wants to arrest Fogg . . .
  1 ☐ in San Francisco.
  2 ☐ in London.
  3 ☐ in New York.

c In San Francisco they have problems . . .
  1 ☐ at the passport office.
  2 ☐ with Fix.
  3 ☐ at a street meeting.

d The Sioux Indians . . .
  1 ☐ stop the train.
  2 ☐ take some passengers away.
  3 ☐ take Passepartout away.

e At Kearney station . . .
  1 ☐ Fix finds Passepartout.
  2 ☐ Fogg looks for Passepartout.
  3 ☐ they get a train to New York.

f When they arrive in New York . . .
  1 ☐ they get a ship to England.
  2 ☐ they are late for the ship.
  3 ☐ they travel by sledge.

WORD WORK

Complete the puzzle. Find the secret word.

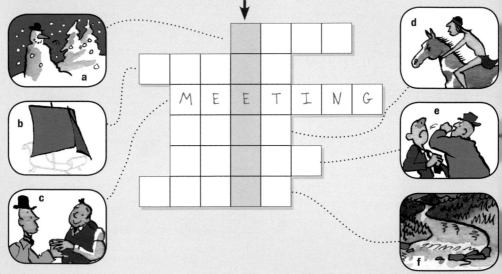

GUESS WHAT

What happens in the next chapter? Tick the boxes.

a The next day they get a ship to . . .

1 ☐ England. **2** ☐ China. **3** ☐ France.

b In Liverpool Fix takes Fogg to . . .

1 ☐ the station. **2** ☐ prison. **3** ☐ a restaurant.

c When Fogg arrives in London he thinks it is . . .

1 ☐

21st Dec

2 ☐

20th Dec

3 ☐

22nd Dec

d Who wins £20,000?

1 ☐

2 ☐

3 ☐

e Who does Mrs Aouda marry?

1 ☐

2 ☐

3 ☐

Chapter 6 The next morning, Fogg, Mrs Aouda, Passepartout and Fix leave on a small ship – the *Henrietta* – going to France.

Later, Fogg gives the **sailors** money, and they **agree** to go to Liverpool – not to France.

The sailors **lock** the **captain** in his room.

The *Henrietta* is in the middle of the Atlantic and there's no **coal**. 'Burn all the **wood** on the ship!' says Fogg.

---

sailor a man who works on a ship

agree to say 'yes'

lock to close with a key

captain the most important sailor on a ship

coal it is black; people use it to make the fire that moves old ships and trains

wood the hard part of a tree

The ship arrives in Queenstown – in the south of Ireland – and there's no more wood on it.

'Let's get off here,' says Fogg to Mrs Aouda, Passepartout and Fix.

Fix doesn't arrest Fogg in Queenstown. He's waiting for them to arrive in England.

They get on a train and travel to Dublin. There they get a fast ship to Liverpool.

In Liverpool Fix arrests Fogg at last, and takes him to prison.

In prison Fogg looks at his **diary**.

At two o'clock he looks at his watch. 'There's time to go to London on a fast train and to be at my club by 8.45 this evening,' he thinks.

At half past three, Fix arrives, with Mrs Aouda and Passepartout.

diary a book where you write about what happens every day

'I'm sorry, Mr Fogg,' says Fix. 'The gentleman thief – James Strand – is in prison. You're free to go!'

Angrily Fogg **punches** Fix in the face.

Then Fogg, Mrs Aouda and Passepartout run to Liverpool station. They get a fast train to London.

LONDON TRAINS

The train arrives at ten minutes to nine. Fogg is five minutes late for his meeting with Stuart.

punch to hit with your closed hand

Fogg doesn't want to get to his club late, so he goes home with Mrs Aouda and Passepartout.

Around the world in eighty days and five minutes – he's the loser! He has only £20,000 in the bank and he must give it all to Stuart.

'I'm sorry for bringing you here, to a **poor** man's home,' he says to Mrs Aouda the next morning. 'Will you **marry** me?' asks Mrs Aouda. 'Yes,' says Fogg.

poor not rich

marry to make someone your husband or wife

36

That afternoon Fogg tells Passepartout. 'I want to marry Mrs Aouda tomorrow, the 23rd December. Can you speak to the people at **Marylebone church** about it?'

Soon Passepartout returns. 'Today's the 21st December. When you travel east around the world you get an extra day. You aren't late for your meeting at the Club after all, but you must run.'

At a quarter to nine Fogg enters his club. 'I win,' he says to Stuart. 'Where's my £20,000?'

Next Monday Fogg – the world-traveller – marries Mrs Aouda. He's a very happy man.

Marylebone /'mɑːlɪbən/

church Christian people go here to pray

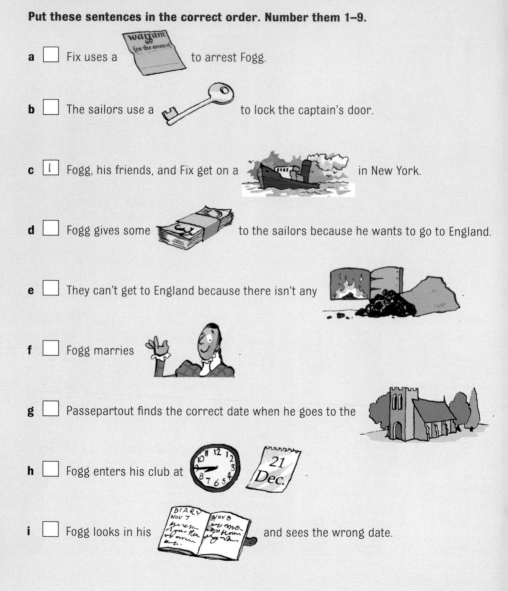

READING CHECK

Put these sentences in the correct order. Number them 1–9.

a ☐ Fix uses a [warrant for the arrest of] to arrest Fogg.

b ☐ The sailors use a [key] to lock the captain's door.

c ☐ Fogg, his friends, and Fix get on a [ship] in New York.

d ☐ Fogg gives some [money] to the sailors because he wants to go to England.

e ☐ They can't get to England because there isn't any [coal].

f ☐ Fogg marries [lady].

g ☐ Passepartout finds the correct date when he goes to the [church].

h ☐ Fogg enters his club at [clock] [21 Dec.].

i ☐ Fogg looks in his [diary] and sees the wrong date.

WORD WORK

Match the words with the pictures.

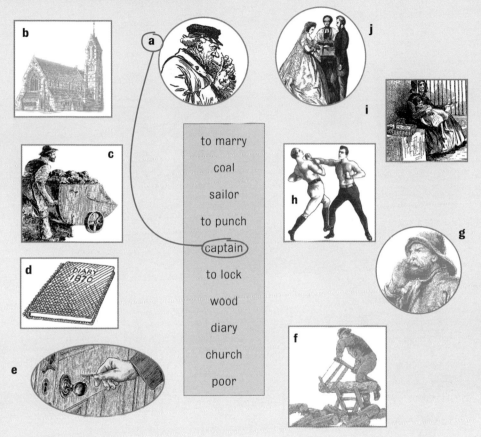

to marry

coal

sailor

to punch

captain

to lock

wood

diary

church

poor

GUESS WHAT

What happens after the story ends?
Answer these questions.

a Are Fogg and Mrs Aouda happy?
b Does Passepartout stay and work for them?
c What happens to Detective Fix?
d Does Fogg ever travel again?

Project A

Postcards from Fix

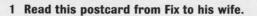

1 Read this postcard from Fix to his wife.

Dear Mabel,

Here we are in Paris. On the front of this postcard you can see a picture of Notre Dame. I like French onion soup. French wine is very good, too. We're leaving tonight for Italy by train.

Perhaps I can write again from Italy.

Love,

Fix

2 **Write this postcard again, with punctuation.**

Dear Mabel Here we are in Italy On the front of this postcard you can see a picture of the Colosseum I like Italian spaghetti Italian wine is very good too Were leaving tonight for Suez by ship Perhaps I can write again from Egypt Love Fix

Dear Mabel,

3 **Write another postcard that Fix sends to Mabel later in the story. Use the postcards above to help you.**

Project B

TRAVEL

1 Draw Fogg's route around the world on the map.

2 **Which five places around the world would you like to visit? Why?**
Use a dictionary to help you.

New York, the USA

The Amazon, Brazil

Sydney, Australia

The South Pole

London, England

Mount Everest, Nepal

Place	Why?
New York, the USA	to learn American English

3 Plan your world trip. Go east. Use an atlas.

ROUTE

from London to Paris

TRANSPORT

by train and boat

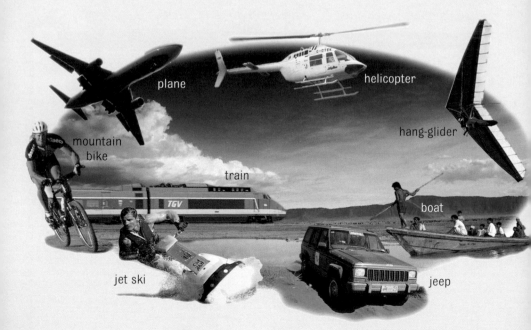

plane

helicopter

hang-glider

mountain bike

train

boat

jet ski

jeep

GRAMMAR CHECK

Linkers: and, but, and or

and links two parts of a sentence with the same idea.

They take a train to Italy and a ship to Egypt.

but links two parts of a sentence with different ideas.

He visits the temple, but he doesn't take off his shoes.

or links another possibility.

Would you like to come with us or would you like to stay here?

1 Write longer sentences using *and*, *but*, or *or* and the sentences in the box.

Fix stays in Bombay.   ~~at midnight he goes home.~~   he runs away from the temple.
he takes him to prison.   he must pay Stuart £20,000.   Fogg doesn't see him.
is he too poor?   the detective buys lots of drinks.   Fix can't arrest him.

a In the evening Fogg eats at his club *and at midnight he goes home.*

b The priests take Passepartout's shoes ....

c Fogg and Passepartout get on the train to Calcutta ....

d Fogg must be back in London by 21st December ....

e In Calcutta Fix is in court ....

f Passepartout doesn't want to help Fix, ...

g Fogg must be in England ....

h In Liverpool Fix arrests Fogg ....

i Does Mrs Aouda want to marry Fogg ....

GRAMMAR

GRAMMAR CHECK

Prepositions of time

Prepositions of time tell you *when* something happens. Study the boxes.

at	in	on
12 o'clock	1810	Sunday
half past ten	October	25th October
8.15 p.m.	the morning / afternoon /	the 14th of June
night	evening	
midnight / midday	two minutes / one hour …	

2 Write *at*, *in*, or *on*.

a .on. 11th November

b ...... midnight

c ...... Thursday morning

d ...... 6.30 a.m.

e 1856

f ...... December 1872

g ...... a quarter past eight

h ...... the afternoon

3 Complete the sentences with *at*, *in*, or *on*.

a Fogg goes around the world ..in. 1872.

b Fogg leaves London .... October.

c He eats at his club .... 12 o'clock.

d Mr Fix sees Fogg in Egypt .... the 9th of October.

e The *Carnatic* leaves Hong Kong .... the evening.

f Fogg and Mrs Aouda want to get on the ship .... the morning.

g Their ship leaves for San Francisco .... a few hours.

h .... six o'clock .... the evening they all go to the American ship.

i They arrive in San Francisco .... the morning.

j The New York train leaves .... the evening.

k Fogg wants to marry Mrs Aouda .... the 23rd of December.

GRAMMAR CHECK

Present Simple: affirmative and negative

To make most Present Simple affirmative verbs we use infinitive without *to*.

Today's detectives move fast.   *I need some new shirts.*

With *he/she/it* we add –s or –es.

Phileas Fogg lives in London.   *He goes to his club every day.*

To make most Present Simple verbs negative we use don't (do not) + infinitive without *to*.

They don't go by plane.   *We don't know where the ship is.*

With *he/she/it* we use doesn't (does not) + infinitive without *to*.

He doesn't take off his shoes.   *She doesn't get into the fire.*

4 **Read Fix's report about Phileas Fogg. Rewrite the sentences changing the verbs from affirmative to negative, or negative to affirmative.**

> a. Fogg is the gentleman thief.
>
> b. He works at a Gentleman's Club in London.
>
> c. Fogg doesn't like eating at his club.
>
> d. Passepartout comes from England.
>
> e. Fogg doesn't read The Times.
>
> f. Fogg and Passepartout want to go around the world in 60 days.
>
> g. They don't like travelling by ship.
>
> h. Passepartout wants to marry Mrs Aouda.

a Fogg isn't the gentleman thief.

b ....

c ....

d ....

e ....

f ....

g ....

h ....

GRAMMAR

GRAMMAR CHECK

Indefinite pronouns: people, things and places

We use these instead of nouns.

people	things	places
someone	*something*	*somewhere*
no one	*nothing*	*nowhere*
everyone	*everything*	*everywhere*

Fogg sees something interesting in The Times. (an interesting thing, but we don't know what)

Fix follows them everywhere. (to all the places they go)

No one sees Passepartout in the fire. (not one person)

5 Complete the sentences with an indefinite pronoun from the box.

someone	~~something~~	somewhere	no one	nothing
nowhere	everyone	everything	everywhere	

a Mrs Aouda is buying ...<u>something</u>... new.

b Passepartout is .... on the *Carnatic* when Fogg looks for him.

c Fix wants to arrest .... in Egypt.

d Passepartout must be .... in Yokohama.

e There is .... in the ticket office so I can't buy a ticket.

f What different things do you need? Have you got .... in your bag?

g They look .... on the ship for Passepartout.

h .... on the *Henrietta* helps Fogg because of his money.

i Fogg can do .... when he goes to prison.

GRAMMAR CHECK

Prepositions of movement

Prepositions of movement tell us how something moves.

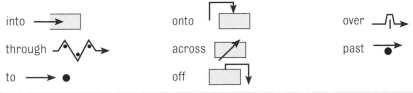

into ⟶

onto

over

through

across

past

to ⟶ ●

off

6 **Complete the story of the train ride from San Francisco to New York.**

They go a) ..to. the station and get b) .... the train in the evening. The train
goes c) .... an old bridge. The bridge falls down d) .... the river. Some
Indians ride e) .... the train. Passepartout gets f) .... the train to fight
and the Indians take him away. Fogg, Mrs Aouda, and Fix get off the train at the next
station. Fogg walks to find Passepartout. Fix finds a sledge with sails and they travel
g) .... the snow with it. In Omaha they take a train h) .... New York.

7 **How do Fogg, Passepartout, and Mrs Aouda travel to Allahabad? Look at the map
and complete the text with the correct prepositions from the Grammar Check box.**

Fogg, Passepartout, and the princess climb a) onto the elephant quickly. The
elephant walks away from Kholby and goes b) .... some trees. Then it walks
c) .... a big river. Near Allahabad they go d) .... a beautiful temple.
But they don't stop, they want to get e) .... Allahabad quickly. The elephant
walks f) .... the railway and g) .... Allahabad. They all get
h) .... the elephant outside a hotel.

GRAMMAR

GRAMMAR CHECK

Present Continuous for future

We can use the Present Continuous to talk about definite future plans.

We form the Present Continuous with the verb be + –ing.

+ *'We're leaving for France,' Fogg tells Passepartout.*

− *'We aren't going to France,' Fogg tells the sailors.*

? *'Are you going around the world?' Yes, I am.*

8 Complete the conversation with the Present Continuous form of the verbs in brackets.

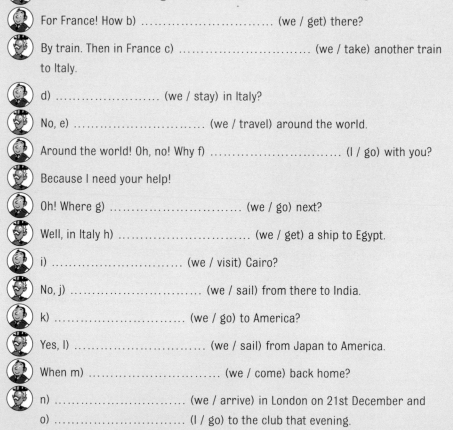

a) ...We're leaving... (we / leaving) for France this evening.

For France! How b) .... (we / get) there?

By train. Then in France c) .... (we / take) another train to Italy.

d) .... (we / stay) in Italy?

No, e) .... (we / travel) around the world.

Around the world! Oh, no! Why f) .... (I / go) with you?

Because I need your help!

Oh! Where g) .... (we / go) next?

Well, in Italy h) .... (we / get) a ship to Egypt.

i) .... (we / visit) Cairo?

No, j) .... (we / sail) from there to India.

k) .... (we / go) to America?

Yes, l) .... (we / sail) from Japan to America.

When m) .... (we / come) back home?

n) .... (we / arrive) in London on 21st December and

o) .... (I / go) to the club that evening.

50

GRAMMAR

GRAMMAR CHECK

Time clauses with before, after, and when

before links a later action with an earlier action.

Fix sends a telegram to London before he gets on the ship for Bombay.

after links an earlier action with a later action.

After Passepartout visits the temple, the priests take his shoes.

when links two actions close in time.

When their ship arrives in Suez, a detective is waiting for them.

We can put *before*, *after*, and *when* clauses at the start of the sentence or at the end.

When we write the time clause first, we must use a comma.

9 Do you remember the story? Complete the sentences with *before*, *after*, or *when*.

a Fix first sees Fogg ..when.. he visits the passport office in Suez.

b .... Passepartout meets Fix in Suez, he goes to buy some shirts.

c Fogg goes to the passport office in Bombay .... he eats at the station.

d Fogg buys some clothes for the princess .... they arrive in Allahabad.

e They get onto the ship for Hong Kong .... they leave the court.

f .... Fogg arrives in Japan, he looks for Passepartout.

g Fogg and Mrs Aouda go to the circus .... their ship leaves for America.

10 Finish the sentences with details from the story. Read the pages in brackets again if you can't remember the story. There may be more than one possible answer.

a When they arrive in Suez, ...Fogg goes to the passport office......
(page 5)

b Before Fogg and Passepartout meet the princess, ...
.... (page 10)

c After they help the princess, ... (page 11)

d When they arrive at Calcutta station, ... (page 15)

e After Passepartout meets Fix at the ticket office in Hong Kong, ...
.... (page 17)

f Before they get the train in San Francisco, ...
.... (page 27)

DOMINOES
THE STRUCTURED APPROACH TO READING IN ENGLISH

Dominoes is an enjoyable series of illustrated classic and modern stories in four carefully graded language stages – from Starter to Three – which take learners from beginner to intermediate level.

Each *Domino* reader includes:

- **a good story** to read and enjoy
- **integrated activities** to develop reading skills and increase active vocabulary
- **personalized projects** to make the language and story themes more meaningful
- **seven pages of grammar activities** for consolidation.

Each *Domino* pack contains a reader, plus a MultiROM with:

- **a complete audio recording of the story**, fully dramatized to bring it to life
- **interactive activities** to offer further practice in reading and language skills and to consolidate learning.

If you liked this Starter Level *Domino*, why not read these?

Journey to the Centre of the Earth
Jules Verne

In Hamburg, Germany, Professor Otto Lidenbrock comes home with an old Icelandic book. In it there is a message about a journey to the centre of the Earth. This is the beginning of one of Jules Verne's most exciting stories.

'Is this message true? We must go to Iceland and see!' says Lidenbrock excitedly. But his nephew, Axel, wants to stay at home.

Can Lidenbrock and Axel – and their Icelandic guide, Hans – find the centre of the Earth? And can they all get back alive after their many underground adventures?

Book ISBN: 978 0 19 424718 4
MultiROM Pack ISBN: 978 0 19 424682 8

The Tempest
William Shakespeare

Prospero, the Duke of Milan, and his daughter Miranda are far away from home, alone on an island in the middle of the Mediterranean Sea. They want to return to Milan . . .

Then, one day Prospero sees a ship near the island carrying his greatest enemies. Prospero, with the help of his magic and the island spirit, Ariel, makes a magic storm – a tempest – to bring them to the island.

Book ISBN: 978 0 19 424707 8
MultiROM Pack ISBN: 978 0 19 424671 2

You can find details and a full list of books in the *Dominoes* catalogue and Oxford English Language Teaching Catalogue, and on the website: www.oup.com/elt

Teachers: see www.oup.com/elt for a full range of online support, or consult your local office.

	CEFR	Cambridge Exams	IELTS	TOEFL iBT	TOEIC
Level 3	B1	PET	4.0	57-86	550
Level 2	A2–B1	KET-PET	3.0-4.0	–	–
Level 1	A1–A2	YLE Flyers/KET	3.0	–	–
Starter & Quick Starter	A1	YLE Movers	–	–	–